BLOOD, SWEAT AND FISTS

STORIES FROM THE PITS

EDITED BY WEASEL

Blood, Sweat and Fists
Stories from the Pits

EDITOR: Weasel

ISBN-13: 978-1-948712-73-6

Copyright © 2020 Weasel

Cover image and design by Weasel

All written and visual works remain the sole property of their creators. They are free to use their works however they see fit.

Printed in the U.S.A.

Weasel Press
Lansing, MI
http://www.weaselpress.com

ALL RIGHTS RESERVED. This book contains material protected under International and Federal Copyright Laws and Treaties. Any unauthorized reprint or use of this material is prohibited. No part of this book, or use of characters in this book, may be reproduced or transmitted in any form or by any means, electronic or mechanical, including photocopying, recording, or by any information storage and retrieval system without express written permission from the authors / publisher.

CONTENTS

My First True Hardcore Show
    Giana LaSpina   9

The Weirdos at The Whiskey in '78
    Nicholas Karavatos   14

Passing Rage Like Communion
    Weasel   17

The King's Klatch
    Mike Fiorito   21

Last Exit
    Nicola Humphreys   28

A Bloody Elegy
    Michael Allen Potter   31

Wig Out at The Ritz
    Jason O'Toole   36

The Mosh Pit
    PoetKen Jones   42

The Night that Killed the Band
    Neil S Reddy   46

Concerts are a pinnacle moment in life. They're a crazy party you go to, get drunk, thrash, fight, or just enjoy the music. I can't count how many shows I've been to, but I've got the concert tickets for most of them. My first being Alice Cooper at Astroworld, Houston, TX 1998. Astroworld is dead and gone now, but I hear the city is talking about reviving it due to renewed interest. I would see Alice several times in Houston, among other bands, but never at Astroworld until 2008 where he played on the dead grounds of what is now a Houston relic. Rock the Bayou Festival had rented the shut down theme park grounds for their 4 day show, and even though a strong hurricane was approaching from the gulf, the festival never shut down.

When you go to a concert, you get an experience. I mean there's the band, but then there's all the other fun and sometimes jackasses that are around you. Some of the best moments in my life happened at a metal show.

This brief anthology is a collection of experiences from concerts. From first time shows to even a member from the band telling their war story. Whatever shit went down for these folks has been put up and bound in these pages.

As you read these stories from the pits, try not to get punched in the face.

Weasel
The Dude

BLOOD, SWEAT AND FISTS

STORIES FROM THE PITS

MY FIRST TRUE HARDCORE SHOW
GIANA LASPINA

Feb. 28, 2018 — Terror, Knocked Loose — The End — Nashville, TN

My first true hardcore show was when I was in seventh grade. My dad had just gotten me into hardcore through Sick of It All, so he surprised me, by taking me to see Terror. This was the first time I had experienced a true hardcore show, and it would spark my love of hardcore and make Terror one of my favorite hardcore bands.

The show was at our local punk club here in Nashville, called the End. This was a CBGB[1]'s type of place: stickers and graffiti everywhere,

---

1. A club in NY where many punk and other type of rock bands got their start.

a bad, beer smell and disgusting, paint-covered tagged bathrooms. I didn't know what to think at first. To be honest I was repulsed, but it grew on me quick. The show was packed, and people were milling about everywhere. To a girl who had just turned thirteen, this was a bit much, so I suggested that we go look at t-shirts.

We made our way over to the raised platform where bands were selling their merchandise and stopped at Terror's booth which was nestled away in the corner. There weren't any other people there because everyone else was looking at Knocked Loose's booth. We approached the booth and the guy manning it greeted us, striking up a conversation. He tells my father and I that he had made a real-life fanzine. We looked at it and ended up purchasing one. Throughout the conversation, I kept thinking to myself, "This guy looks really familiar. But *why*?" When my dad and I picked out our shirts, my dad says that it's my first real show and the guy looked at me, promising that it will be great. And then it dawned on me. I am talking to Scott Vogel, the singer of Terror. I was kind of startled because he was the only famous person I'd ever met at that point. He was really, really nice. I was so psyched to meet him.

So the show starts and the local band goes up, and then the next band, Year of the Knife comes up. They announced themselves as a straight-edge band from Delaware. I pay special attention to them, not just because I'm straight edge, but also because their bassist is a girl. She blew me away.

After Year of the Knife comes Jesus Piece, and they were pretty good too. After them, my dad and I sat on the stage, and we waited until Terror came on. The lights dim, they walk out, and we all cheer. My mind is blown. They are this hurricane of force and exhilaration that I cannot comprehend. I watched the pit, knowing soon it'll be my turn. After they finish the first song, Scott tells the crowd to get moving, and my dad throws me on to the stage, which is about two feet tall, and tells me to dive onto my back. I follow his instructions, and it turns out that it is so much fun to me. I get into the pit, and my body automatically knows what to do. I already know that the windmills and spin-kicks are lame, and that they *hurt*. Like, really badly; and to keep it moving. So I do, and when the song ends, the next one starts, and then stops abruptly.

We looked at the stage, where Scott spoke into the mike.

"Some of the sound is out."

While we wait for the crew to fix it, Scott talked to us about punk stuff, and specifically the documentary *Another State of Mind*, and how he loved Minor Threat. Then he made us sing Stick Tight with him, all of us. The whole crowd who knew it sang it.

Eventually the sound got fixed, and Scott decided he was going to tell specific people to get onstage. He looked around and pointed at me, and the girl next to me.

"You girls," he says. "You'll get up here. Ready?"

We look at him, and as the song starts, my dad came behind us and threw us both onstage. We go and go, and everyone in the crowd was having a great time. Unfortunately, they finished their set and bid us farewell. I followed my dad outside past the smoker's courtyard, and sat by the front door. I was sweaty, and hot, and I felt like I was going to puke. We chugged our waters and waited for Knocked Loose to start, and I turned to my dad.

"Have you ever heard of these guys?"

My dad said yes, that they were a metalcore band from the Louisville area. A shirt we bought of theirs, a long-sleeved one, said Oldham County on the back, which is where they're from in Kentucky.

We both decided we were tired, and that pit time was over now that we'd seen Terror. So we ascended to the raised viewing platform where people who didn't want to be in the pit could watch. In reality it is the same height as the stage, it just has a guardrail in front of it. So we go up there and stand at the guardrail, tiredly watching. They come out, and their singer greets us with a "WHAT THE HECK IS

UP NASHVILLE!" The crowd went wild. When Knocked Loose was playing, you could feel the tiny building shake and sway due to the motion of the crowd. They were a frenetic energy that exploded into release. The band was all over the stage, and the crowd was all over the place too. After their set, I decided that I would for sure check these guys out, they were that good. And I did. They were great.

For a first show, this was probably the greatest I was ever going to get outside of New York; and I couldn't have hoped for anything different. This show changed me completely, and it made me realize that hardcore was something I wanted to be a part of. The intensity that is Terror is something I have experienced one time after this, but it was nothing like being crammed into a tiny room with 200 other sweaty people. Overall, it was an enlightening and eye-opening experience that I will never forget.

THE WEIRDOS AT THE WHISKEY IN '78
NICHOLAS KARAVATOS

The Weirdos—The Whiskey A-Go-Go, Sunset Blvd.—Hollywood, California

Longhair teen beach boy in the late '70s likes Black Sabbath and Grateful Dead concerts. Tickets are easy to get and not expensive. But I am looking for something else, too, and an older friend takes me to The Weirdos and The Dils at The Whiskey.

These are more pogo days than mosh days, but it's a pit.

We are up front at the stage. A short thick woman pushes me aside to stand at the stage. She's dressed in black, leathery, shades of blue in her spikey hair. The Weirdos come on and she raises her arms and howls in delight. She turns around, locks eyes with me, raises her arms in the air and howls. I return the smile, nod in affirmation, and she turns back to the band, bouncing in enjoyment.

I look behind me. A tall man dressed in black plastic trash bags adhered to his body with electrical tape. I look up, and our eyes meet and I nod, I look down, and turn back to the band. Behind me he quakes and quivers with The Weirdos in enjoyment.

A smartly though not inappropriately dressed photographer stands to my left, a little more centerstage. My friend's older brother takes it upon himself to gentlemanly block for her. She was not of the audience. With our long blond hair, she looks like a city-me and is enjoying herself.

Beach boy is wearing shoes, old blue jeans and a plain white t-shirt.

I watch a guitar player in torn painter's pants. I wonder if that's his day-job or if it's a dumpster score.

The sweating singer sits on a monitor: "And now for my next composition..." I expected an attitude of decomposition and, wherever his tongue actually is, I enjoy this calm, mill-runner intro. And then the song: *We've got it!*

The churn of the spiral had not yet become the essence of the pit.

I am jostled by free-formality, pogo and

proto-mosh dust devils, but I am not aggressed. I am catharsed. I stand and watch and listen in joy.

Like the possible (or not) *I-take-myself-seriously-even-if-you-don't* introduction to "We've Got the Neutron Bomb," the cultural sophistication of the moment is a Dadaist correction to the music on the radio. The wellbeing of a little puking is the blood that waters.

This is how I lived my first night in the pit.

PASSING RAGE LIKE COMMUNION WEASEL

July 18, 2000—Maximum Rock:Anthrax/Motley Crue/Megadeth—Cynthia Woods Mitchell Pavillion—Woodlands, TX.

I was eleven years old. I remember my dad got the tickets for free. Kiss was coming the next month, all four original members gearing up for their "Farewell Tour." We all know the history of that now. Some things don't die when they need to.

Ticketmaster ran a promotion. Purchase the Kiss tickets and get access to the Maximum Rock tour. The sales were down, but looking back, smashing Motley Crue between Anthrax and Megadeth wasn't the best idea for a tour. Let's be real, you can't mosh to Girls, Girls, Girls, and Megadeth ain't known for their ballads.

2000 was the year of lackluster releases. Risk came out the year before and Megadeth didn't bother to play anything from it. Anthrax stuck to their hits, but they wouldn't have a new album until 2003. Motley Crue had New Tattoo and were the only band to play a new song. Not that it'd go noticed.

The sun had just started to descend as Anthrax hit the stage. There were more people on the lawn than in the seats of the Pavilion. The hill erupted into war as bodies smashed into each other. A mesh of long, matted hair flew through the weak breeze as people rolled to the bottom. Moshing while drunk on a hill is a skill not many can master.

I always felt the Pavilion never needed to water the lawn with the amount of beer that was tossed over it. As Anthrax moved through their short setlist, beer rained down like a Texas hurricane. The winds from the mass circle pit, rain from the plastic cups sold at unreal prices by marching band kids, and hail from the ice created an atmosphere of drunk destruction. My first introduction to Anthrax was that of chaos and madness encased in an outdoor asylum, and I loved every moment of it.

Before Motley Crue took the stage, security came to the lawn and announced that we could move into the seats. There wasn't a large enough audience and the band needed to stroke their ego in order to have a good show. We moved up, but it didn't matter. The audience had moved out of the area to get more beer and talk. Why watch some hair metal band after being assaulted by a group who could destroy the stage? There was no pit this time around. The first ballad that formed in the air put most of the crowd to sleep. By the fourth or fifth song, most of us had wanted Anthrax to return for an encore before being demolished by Megadeth.

The moment Megadeth blasted Holy Wars...Punishment is Due, we woke again. Most of us moved back to the lawn and formed another circle pit. I've always had a love/hate relationship with Dave Mustaine. The mesh of his homophobia through his faith and him being a general asshole pushed me far away from some of Megadeth's best music. Peace Sells is a classic, but feeling alienated by the lead ain't something I need to feel as a fan.

He didn't interact much with the crowd that night. Like the rest of the line-up, he was there to play his set and leave. It's hard to get excited about doing a show when you're attendance is lackluster at best. And though it was dark, you could still see the empty seats.

Mustaine played with fury. His guitar raged through his set. His Symphony of Destruction demolished us. Face filled with disdain, he showed us his war was far worse than what we had started in our own raging mosh. We still devoured ourselves. What else to do except pass the rage to each other like communion?

When he finished, he took his rage with him. A calm settled over us, a few cries for more, but the rest left to the mosquitoes as we left.

THE KING'S KLATCH, 1980, L'AMOUR, BROOKLYN, NY, KING DIAMOND
MIKE FIORITO

1980 — King Diamond — L'Amour — Brooklyn, NY

I'll admit that I wasn't a heavy metal fan, but our friend, Joe, insisted that we had to see King Diamond. This was 1980.

"This is great music, man." He said. "They're amazing musicians. It's not just guitar shredding."

"What's the band's name again?" asked Lan.

"King Diamond," said Joe with a straight face.

Lan and I laughed.

"Trust me," pleaded Joe, shaking his head affirmatively to underscore the seriousness of the band and his opinion of them.

But Lan and I were doubtful. Our love of heavy metal music stopped at Black Sabbath and Deep Purple, but Joe was deep into groups like Megadeth, Iron Maiden and Motorhead. He had the albums, wore their t-shirts. Lan and I were more into progressive and psychedelic rock, groups like Yes, Jethro Tull and King Crimson. Psychedelic groups wrote songs about other worlds, about the love of the universe, of knowledge. That kind of crap. They transported us out of the drab Long Island City world that we grew up in, factory and project buildings, and placed us into new fantastic realms. The album covers were fairytale-like. A chunk of earth floating out into space. Extraterrestrial creatures. And the instruments they played. And played them well. Mandolins, acoustic guitars. Moog synthesizers. Spacey far out shit. Somewhere between *Lord of the Rings* and *Star Trek*. This is where we wanted to be. Lost in the cosmic swirl. Not stuck in the dismal shithole of the projects, or in the satanic hellhole of Heavy Metal.

But Joe persisted. He begged. Let's face it, he didn't want to go alone - all the way to L'Amour in Bay Ridge, Brooklyn from Queens. And he wanted us to like his music, too.

We had to take the train to 62nd Street in

Brooklyn. To make the long train ride bearable, we smoked a joint in between the train cars. We held onto the train handles, passing a joint with our free hand, swaying with the stopping and starting of the train. The great thing about riding in-between train cars was that you could do anything. You could smoke cigarettes, pee on the tracks, or vomit into the rushing air if you had to. This was the NYC subway system. There were no rules.

Before we went back into the train car, Lan and I popped a hit of mescaline. Joe never took drugs. He just watched us as we slowly devolved into idiots.

Sitting in the train car, we laughed and joked. The train moved slowly, creaking its way to Brooklyn. There was garbage swirling around the train cars and graffiti on the train walls. As littered and filthy as the train car looked, it began to glow and shimmer.

By the time we got to our stop, the mescaline and weed had fully kicked in. Walking down the street you could hear the buzzing of the neon signs, like they were speaking to you in some secret electronic language, luring you into the stores upon which they hung. Maybe there were aliens hiding behind the counters in the stores.

From the outside, L'Amour looked like a humdrum bar, but when the door swung open, the bright velvet curtains and ornate chandeliers gave the impression that you stepped into a medieval dungeon. The mescaline was now fully pumping through my brain. The colors were sharper and the sounds were more articulated. I could hear wind in the drum cymbals and radar signals in the guitar notes.

There were at least three floors inside the club and little alcoves with couches where you could make-out or smoke weed in a more private place. Since the band hadn't yet started, we roamed around the club exploring its hidden chambers.

The castle-like atmosphere was enhanced by the chalky white-faced zombie fans that sashayed through the venue. The dead look in their eyes was a little ominous. Along with the now thundering guitar sounds and heavy bass riffs pounding the walls, it felt like we were secretly being led into a slaughter. Machines blew out curls of smoke that twirled and twisted in the arena lights, taking on the changing colors. There were lights flashing and blinking to the music. The only thing that was missing was lightening and rain.

Style-wise, Joe, Lan and I were completely out of place here. We wore simple dungaree pants and t-shirts. We didn't have gothic outfits, make-up or long purple fingernails. And our hair was more afro-like than long.

Suddenly all attention turned toward center

stage. It became completely dark and suddenly very silent. The zombies gathered around us; I wondered if they would try to eat us in a savage frenzy.

Then the lights flooded the stage. The band, as if materializing out of nowhere, began playing. The music sounded like the groan of a gigantic metallic whale chained to a cage in hell.

As the thick smoke from the stage cleared, a bejeweled coffin emerged from the blackness. I could hear grunting from the zombies around me. Were they alive, or were they dead already. Mouths open, hands now extended, they eagerly waited for the moment their leader would tear into them, like a devil released from Hell, ripping open their stomachs with his fangs and claws.

Joe kept pointing to the stage. He was whispering to me and Lan, but we couldn't hear him.

We wanted to laugh but between the mescaline and the weed, we were scared out of our wits. I swear I could see bats flying around us. This was getting serious now.

And then, the coffin slowly opened. The leader of the dead zombies, King Diamond, stepped out of the coffin. He stuck his tongue out and made threatening faces, opening his mouth wide, pushing his eyeballs out of his head.

As soon as he started singing, the zombies began shaking their long hair in unison with thudding rhythms, as if their hair was clapping to the music. Shaking their skulls likely also made their brains turn into a mushy pulp.

We just stood in awe, our hands by our sides.

Singing into a microphone shaped like a human skull, King Diamond's face was painted with blood, as if his zombie worshippers had chewed into his cheeks. At some point, King Diamond's body seemed to spin and whirl to the music. The stage was now a vortex where demonic wizards and spirits swam in an embryonic cell. Their bodies liquefied and oozed in the placental walls, their essences melting to the hypnotic rhythms and screaming guitar frequencies. This was way beyond just music. This was a consecrated transfiguration. Like we were witnessing the beating heart of the universe, everything that had ever lived and died. All existences metamorphosing into a single blood cell that pulsed and pumped. It was nothing short of a possession.

On the train ride home, we were followed by goblins and demons. Some of them were disguised as ordinary passengers. We kept moving to different cars to escape them and because we couldn't stop laughing. And every time we stopped laughing we got serious, concerned that some evil spirit would attack us with spikes and toss our severed limbs to other flesh-eating fiends. We weren't sure if the train was going down into Hell or just west and north back to Queens.

Somehow we made it home, stumbling back to the Ravenswood project building we lived in. It was almost three in the morning. A pink sliver streaked the sky, suggesting that the world would be once again rested from the demons.

LAST EXIT
NICOLA HUMPHREYS

Fields of the Nephilim — Leeds Poly, UK

8 May 1988.
Fields of the Nephilim were playing one of my most-frequented venues, Leeds Poly, UK. I may as well have gone there alone, for I spent every gig holding his wallet, while he bounded like a puppy straight on into the middle of the action. He'd return sweaty and ragged, with the exhausted swagger of a man after battle. My perfect spot was (obviously) next to the mixing desk, where I used to hang out with my goth friends Graham (the concert bootlegger) and Hazel, his girlfriend of many hair colors. I'd occasionally see glimpses of my boyfriend

as he jumped from the stage or was held in place, standing up, perfectly balanced on someone's shoulders. His arms stretched out to the sides like Christ the Redeemer. He'd fall spectacularly, then climb right back up there again. This night, however, was very different. The bravado of youth was not prepared for the wooden clog sole of a New Model Army (NMA) fan hitting his skull.

I saw him half-dragged, half-carried from the crowd, drenched in a mixture of sticky flour and blood. His adrenaline kicked in and he had to be persuaded not to go back into the pit. Reluctantly, we ran down the road to the hospital where they treated him more swiftly than he probably should have been. This was most likely due to his determination to leave as soon as possible. Half a dozen medical students watched as a lock of his long hair was cut close to his scalp, and some form of superglue applied. No stitches or kept in for observation. Face wiped clean, the obligatory light shone to check his pupils, job done. We ran back to the venue, but the doors were locked.

25 August 1998.
The not-so-secret, pre-festival gig at The Majestic in Reading, UK was the next chance we had to see Fields of The Nephilim. Some of The Militia (NMA fans) recognized my boyfriend and were relieved to see he was fighting fit.

The next day, Fields of The Nephilim played the Reading Festival, where my boyfriend was again bashed on the head by a stage diving fan's boot. Passed out, he was carried over strangers heads, then dragged over the barrier by Security. I didn't even know he had been injured, until I finally found him, about three hours later. He was shocked and pale, drinking orange squash, enjoying the hospitality of a St John's Ambulance tent. Whether it was his decision, or my begging through anxious tears, his days of being part of a human pyramid in the mosh pit were over. All he had left was the Salvation t-shirt he was wearing both times. That t-shirt should have been thrown away, but he had persuaded his mum to wash it so the blood stains were permanently fixed into the fabric. A badge of honor.

I wonder if he went bald and wears that scar with pride.

A BLOODY ELEGY
MICHAEL ALLEN POTTER

Nov. 3rd, 1992 — The Rollins Band — Metropolis, Montréal, QC,

I took a Greyhound, round-trip overnight, from Schenectady to Montréal to see the show (because all of the other dates on the East Coast had already sold out). I'd seen Henry Rollins once before, fronting Black Flag, when they'd toured with Painted Willy and Gone about a decade prior, but this felt different because I'd come out in the interim and my need to see Hank at the helm of his new outfit was visceral, a physical ache, that was really tough to explain to anyone at the time.

I'd been to Metropolis once (or twice?)

before and remembered that they had a strict dress code. There was no way that I was going to spend hours on a bus to get dinged on a technicality at the door, so I wore a jacket and tie (both secondhand or thrifted) to guarantee entry to the massive space (it was palatial and Eurostylish and made exponentially more remarkable because it was just over the border which, from my provincial perspective at the time, delineated unrelenting boredom from total fucking French-accented big-city excitement).

Rollins was on tour (with his eponymous new band) with Da Lench Mob and the Beastie Boys (in support of *Check Your Head*) and the Rollins Band was second on the bill, but the sole reason that I'd made this particular pilgrimage. When I got to the club, the line was wrapped around the block and when I got in it, I was informed (almost immediately) that my presence was unwelcome. How did I know this? Because I was surrounded by punks in standard regalia (leather/pins/patches/chains/Mohawks/lager) who screamed at me in a Québécois so guttural that it sounded like German. I stood my ground, though, folding my arms across my (unfortunately) button-downed chest and lifting me chin in defiance of the man shouting an inch from my face as others circled like smaller sharks, spitting their sartorial disapproval like sloppy punctuation at various points of his extended tirade. I am a fighter by nature (my great-grandfather was a notorious Irish bar-brawler), but I remember thinking *Fuck this uniform bullshit!* but not engaging, not taking the bait from anyone because the stakes (Henry or not-Henry) were far too high.

Needless to say, adrenaline and impatience were coursing through my veins during the opening act. I remember thinking that they were decent, but I couldn't name a song or quote a lyric if you paid me. Somehow, I made it through the interminable hang-time after their set and pushed my way as close as I could when Rollins & Co. finally took to the stage. I was transfixed, enraptured, in awe, ignoring the grind and the aggression of the pit, intent on the tattooed, muscular man in the black shorts who was also ignoring the chaos surrounding him.

Trust me when I tell you that I am a dedicated fan, that music (in one form or another) has saved my life at various times, but I'm not one of those people who takes much note of set lists preferring, instead, to be fully present in the moment that music is being performed in front of me. With that said, I understand the (general) mechanics of a show, the ebb and flow of up-tempo vs. down, new material vs. old(er), and I was thrown that night, not by a bouncer or by a gutter punk, but by a song unfamiliar. I moved closer still, compelled by the intensity of Henry's savagery, got kicked (full on) in the head on my way to the edge of the stage, but I stayed the course, bleeding, never losing sight of the sweat or the pain pouring out of him. I could hear profound loss without actually being able to discern the bulk of the lyrics (above the distortion, the feedback, and the combative decibel levels), save these:

Why/Why am I/Still alive (alive, alive, alive…)?

I'd travelled hundreds of miles over the course of 24 hours to mainline some ferocity that was, essentially, familiar to me, but the song, rather the performance of the song, haunted me for years, even following me out to the West Coast. So I wrote to Henry Rollins from my ramshackle shotgun apartment (above Grooves Records on Market Street in San Francisco) and I asked him, essentially, what I had witnessed that night (because I couldn't find the track, or evidence of the song, anywhere). And he wrote back (let's take a moment here: *holyfuckingshit, he wrote back!*) to tell me that it was murder that I had witnessed. Or, more specifically, its aftermath, as "Hole in the Back of My Mind" was about his friend, Joe Cole, who had been shot and killed during a home invasion in the apartment that they'd shared in Los Angeles. It's on the demo for *The End of Silence* and there's some grainy footage on YouTube (that I watch and I watch and I watch) from a performance in

New York City during which Henry effortlessly throws men offstage who have crawled out of the frenzy (like drunk frat boys crashing a funeral during the eulogy) so that he can continue to shout at a world that can extinguish a life without notice, explanation, or apology.

Photo of Brian Baker provided by Author

WIG OUT AT THE RITZ
JASON O'TOOLE

September 5, 1987 — GBH, Dag Nasty, Murphy's Law and The Accused — The Ritz, NY, NY

"Molly Ringwald, plus one."

"Yup. You're on here. Oh…it's plus four."

Score! I wave over three of my friends and we head inside the venue, The Ritz where England's charged GBH are headlining and a couple of my friend's bands are supporting. Molly is dating one of the Beastie Boys and I had already been told by a classmate who is dating Adam Yauch she is not coming to the show tonight. It seems that everyone else in New York is showing up to The Ritz tonight. Seattle thrash band, The Accused are kicking it off. On next, New York's own Murphy's Law, recently returned from supporting The Beastie Boys on their Licensed to Ill tour. My friends Dag Nasty are rounding out a formidable bill.

Having gone quickly from young fan to fanzine editor, promoter and musician, I got spoiled to not paying for shows – which was convenient as I was pretty much on my own dime going to college in Manhattan. When I wasn't on the guest list and the doorman was a stranger to me, I had a con which worked 100% of the time at the larger venues in the city. I was always the "plus one" for some celebrity, Spin Magazine, or whatever record label I thought of while approaching will call.

Dag Nasty are already there loading in and Brian hands me a metal briefcase full of change for the merch table. I feel like I'm holding the nuclear football for the President. Upstairs, it's pandemonium. Adam Yauch, known to the world as the leather jacket clad "MCA" of the most successful band to emerge from the hardcore scene, is backstage with his girlfriend Aura. Brazen young ladies are throwing themselves at the door to the lounge that is crammed in with all four bands and their friends. Big Charley, an aptly named bouncer both for his physique and his heart, is holding back the mob. He's saving us from being assaulted by the riffraff and chuckling at the silliness of it all. A determined young woman, who looks a bit like the teased out blonde Meg Ryan in Working Girl, wiggles her way past him. Mistaking me for one of the Beastie Boys, she writes her name and number on the sleeve of my vintage varsity jacket, before she is forcibly ejected.

"Oh no. That's permanent marker." says Murphy's Law roadie, Joe Bruno, rubbing at it with a with a fingerless-gloved hand. Joe and I talk about our luck with the ponies up in Saratoga as Big Charley fights back the barfly-zombie apocalypse outside our door. I know Aura from the New School where we are freshmen and strike up a conversation with her and Adam about college. He attended Bard and I had run into him at a Bad Brains gig once before.

"You know, if you play your cards right, I might be able to feature this band of yours in The Plain Truth." This being the photocopied fanzine I wrote with longtime friend, Sam McPheeters. "It could really give your group the exposure you need."

"Wow. Thanks for looking out!" Adam laughs.

Colin Abrahall of GBH is sitting in the corner, half asleep.

"Are you straightedge?" He asks, noting my appearance which could easily be mistaken for Youth Crew. "You should try some speed!" There're more than a few substances being abused in the room.

"You should try putting the speed back in your music." I counter.

The Accused have blazed through their set and Murphy's Law is up. Brian Baker asks me to get the briefcase I'm holding down to the merch table. I can't get out the door that Big Charley is holding closed so I head down to the stage. Chris, the promoter, a squirrelly fellow who looks like a cross between Doug Henning and Kenny G shouts, "Nobody backstage!" grabbing me by the arm.

Reflexively, I slam the briefcase into his stomach and he doubles over. He has two bouncers with him but they seem amused by the situation and stand still while the promoter yells like a cartoon villain. "After him!" A couple of skinhead girls get in between the permed promoter and me, allowing me to escape by stagediving into the crowd, briefcase in hand.

If I tried this move today at age 50, I would probably end up in traction, but I was 18 and as far as I knew at the time, as invincible as I was crazy. I deliver the briefcase to the merch table in time to see Joey Ramone leaving. Standing 6'6" he's an impressive sight, even though I've gotten accustomed to seeing him and his bandmates around town – they never stopped hanging out and played gigs almost every weekend. He's wearing his iconic leather jacket and painted on jeans. Tilting his head all the way back, he drains a can of cheap beer which he tosses over his shoulder before striding out to the sidewalk.

Dag Nasty tear through their set, with Brian at the height of his powers. He's spent his Minor Threat royalties on a wireless transmitter for his guitar and flies around the stage with nothing to tether him down. Singer Peter is connecting with the crowd on an emotional level few can match. They have all but set up the great GBH for failure – as their take on English punk has become more sluggish. It's good stuff but out of sync with the frenzied energy that the opening bands have created in this venue.

As the night's festivities end, we get word that Gentleman Jim, the singer of the NJ straightedge parody band, Crucial Youth is in trouble. Some of the Youth Crew who are lacking the funny gene have promised to give him a beat down outside the club. It's only fitting that Brian Baker, a progenitor of the straightedge movement, has decided to rescue him. He quickly devises an A-Team style operation. With bassist Doug at the wheel of their tour van, and me manning the sliding side door, we pull up in front of The Ritz, just as Brian and Peter race out the front like two Secret Service

Agents, the embattled Crucial Youth frontman between them. I throw open the door, they leap in and we all race off, leaving the humorless hoodied goblins standing on the sidewalk with nobody to throw their fists at.

As I get back to the dorms, I realize that I've got the strangest contact high of my life courtesy of my pals backstage. My face smears in the plate-glass window of the lobby as I pass my reflection. My hands leave sparkling trails as I wave them in front of my face. Between the secondhand smoke of angel dust and formaldehyde cigarettes, along with the natural rush of endorphins, sleep is not going to happen. I sat up with friends in the dorms, as we debriefed each other on a most historic night. This was one of many nights which made New York the greatest Hardcore scene in the world in 1987.

THE MOSH PIT
POETKEN JONES

The first band I was ever in played hardcore punk music. I had been to punk shows before but always tried to stay out of the melee on the floor. At a particularly memorable early 80s show at Club Foot in Austin, Texas, I watched from the balcony as a fan beaned Iggy Pop in the head with a beer bottle, promptly ending the show and causing a mini-riot. I decided after that incident the safest survival strategy was to stay away from the center of the action.

Unfortunately, when you become lead singer of a punk band you ARE the center of the action. Our first few club gigs were with non punk bands so I thought maybe we'd never face the arm swinging body contortions of a full on mosh pit. But I was wrong. Our first headlining gig brought out the skinhead crowd. Not being a Neo-Nazi, I really hadn't given much thought to these guys before, but apparently they were now our fan base.

As we started our opening song, I watched in horror as five or six large skinheads charged at me head on, arms flailing as if in epileptic seizures, pushing me into their midst. Fortunately my good friend George Reul was in the crowd and noticing my discomfort, he got up and launched the most violent skinhead (who I later learned was fucking my girlfriend- -to be fair we were technically broken up but on again, off again--into a stage side table. George is a big man and back then he enjoyed fighting. The skinheads backed away and let us finish the set in physical peace, though on an old tape of the gig I can still hear a guy screaming "Play more thrashers!"

A few years later I moved to LA. My music had matured into a more alternative style, but I still enjoyed going to punk shows. One night my friend and talented Webmaster and Videographer Steve Luksic (you can see his work on the LA Riot music video of my song "Fiddle While It Burns " on my website at www. poetken.com or his Vimeo channel) attended a show in Hollywood. We were standing at the bar when a mosh pit developed by the stage.

"What are they doing?" He asked innocently.

"Dude, that's a mosh pit. It's a punk rock ritual. I hated it when I used to perform"

One point to note here is that Steve is not only a 6 foot five-inch giant (as they used to say about the Yugo he is the cutting edge of Serbo-Croatian engineering) but he also carries an aura of unflappable invincibility.

"I'm going to go check it out" he began to amble toward the seething sweating mass of moshers.

"Be careful" I called after him "they don't kid around in there".

I gulped my beer fearing the worst for Steve. But I watched in utter amazement as he slowly walked right through the heart of the mosh pit totally unfazed. He looked like a cross between a Golem and the Statue of Liberty, holding his camera high in his right hand while numerous skinheads bounced off him like a rubber ball off a wall. I've never seen anything like it before or since. He sauntered back through the crowd and returned to the bar.

"They weren't that bad" he calmly picked up his beer.

"Wow. I've never seen anyone walk through a mosh pit like that! You were like Moses parting the Red Sea"

I don't know if he still has the video of that show but I do know this fact: I'm too damn old to ever consider entering the slam dance fury of a mosh pit again. But I am happy to have survived those adventures and so many more in my halcyon musician youth.

THE NIGHT THAT KILLED THE BAND
NEIL S REDDY

Starting Point of Genocide (SPOG)—Indian Queen—Boston, Lincolnshire[2]

When I tell this story, I always have to say this is a true story and say it twice because nobody ever believes me, but this is a true story. So let's tell it properly, over a couple of beers and late at night. Put on some sounds, sit back and I'll tell it right, just as it was…

---

2. All photos in this piece were provided by the author.

The Venue

The late lamented 'Indian Queen,' a sprawling three story Victorian pub, built for the hard-drinking hard-working folks of Boston, Lincolnshire. That's the original Boston, so bad the American's left it. It was situated at the entrance to Dolphin Lane, a cramped alley just off the town's main square. For twenty years it was a much loved, regularly packed to the gills hard-rock, punk venue. And they came from all over the country, Europe, Canada and the USA to play at the Indian Queen.

Let's step backwards into present time speak and give the place a quick tour. On the ground floor, a saloon bar where the smaller, artsy, midweek bands play. Next floor up—staff quarters, NEVER BOTHER THE STAFF, not if you want to play, leave them alone, they bite—carry on up too more flights until you reach...the venue.

A Victorian dance hall, with a beef brown wooden floor and a proper raised stage. The stage is crammed with a drum kit, a collection of PA's and an assortment of amps abandoned by bands that had to make a quick getaway, if you didn't cut it at the Queen you had to get out quick. Bugger the equipment, they'll eat it. Most nights the stage was so tight everybody, but the drummer had to stand on the dance floor to play—remember that its important.

Those Victorians knew how to build walls

and the bands at the Indian Queen proved this to be true twice a week. We punished those walls with Laney and Marshall Amps turned-up to full crank, and those walls took it. They soaked it up like sweet wine. The sound was amazing. The hall itself smelt like a three-day armpit but it had every right to, after all it had absorbed one hundred years of sweat, spilt pints, cigarette smoke and tears - and a pint of two of blood.

Downstairs again, out the back in the alley is where substances not served on the premises are consumed, unless you're playing in which case you get to use a backroom near the toilets. The toilets need a special mention. They had once been outside, open-air privies and they still thought they were. They occasionally pretended to be swamp land, cultivating its own primitive lifeforms. Graffiti from the fifties had been gaining consciousness and sometimes tried to communicate with the punters, especially if they'd overindulged in the back alley. Grown men feared going in there alone and girls went in by fours. In short, the Indian Queen was the perfect punk venue.

The Band

On the night in question six bands were playing their high-octane noise but the band we're concerned about here was called Starting Point of Genocide, otherwise known as SPOG. Four guys who were old enough to know better. We were second-wave punks who were old enough to remember the first wave, and just couldn't help diving in.

Roll call—Fozz the left-handed drummer whose tattoos were taller than he was and had once played with Hawkwind, a shameful act nobody ever let him forget. Jon the brick-shithouse bass player who tuned his bass so low it aroused elephants. On guitar me, called Agent Red, I knew too many chords to be truly punk but my axe sounded like a pissed-off lion, so I passed muster. (Guitar geek fact—it had also been blessed by the Hernandez Bros of 'Love and Rockets' comics—'Rock on Motherfucker). And then there was Eagle on vocals. Eagle had been on the scene for over twenty years and still had the of a stopped clock but what he lost

in he made up for in showmanship. Old and crumbling but we were the band to beat.

And this is how the band died. Picture this, pre-gig, my cell phone rings. I put down my pint. I hear my partner's teary voice on the end of the line, 'I'm pregnant.'

'What?!'—it's been ten years since our son was born. I've had the snip, I've been the responsible guy. Did I hear that wrong? What did she say—I reached for the pint.

'I'm pregnant!'

I took a gulp of beer, 'it's not mine.'

'What do you mean it's not yours!'

'No, no I've picked up the wrong pint! Honest I picked up the wrong pint,' – honest, really, it's true.

Voice from the stage and next up SPOG!

'It's great, great, we'll be fine. I gotta go play!' End of call—somehow the relationship survived.

Luckily the audience was in a good mood— 'Twats! Fuckers! Eat shit and die! Crucify him!' They were ready for us, keeping them waiting would have been a mistake.

I plugged into a Marshall stack and cranked it, no pedals, no effects, just the amp and a handmade Bare Knuckle War Pig humbucker pick-up, like they gave a shit. It roared and that's all that mattered.

Fozz kicks in the tribal beat and it begins. There was no mosh pit at the Indian Queen,

the dance floor was the mosh pit. If you didn't want to be in it you climbed onto a table or the reclaimed church pews that ran alongside the dance floor, and got out of the way. One choice get out or get in.

Eagle launches in, full scream - a beat too early, but who cares –

Friday night queuing for the pie and chips,
Guy in the apron says it's the pits,
Blacks get the breaks and we get nix.
I say, Oi you! Eat my fist!
Chip Shop Fascist! That's all I fucking need!
Chip Shop Fascist!
That's all I fucking need! What made him think I'd agree!

And already they're singing along. Punching the air as they stamp and stomp in an ever-deceasing circle that ends in a fist swinging multiple pile up—wait for it—MOSH!

It's on, the room is riot and rave, animal fury and joyous abandon. Front and center the Lincolnshire lasses who don't take no shit from nobody and certainly won't take it from no meathead man, they're swinging fists, handbags and hairbrushes to the beat. To the left the young guns flaying each other with haymaker punches and karate kicks. To the right the old guard, pogo, pogo, pogo and toss in a beer or two. At the back, a growing pile of

all-in grapple wrestlers are shaking out each other's teeth. It's a good night.

Second song, Jon's bass ripples the air. The pulse passes through flesh, grabs the backbone and says BOOM! The room moves as one now. We've reached hive mentality. Band and audience moving as one. The floor bends with the bounce, The tables move, chairs topple but the those fucking old walls hold. We are the motion, we are the sound — it's a thing of beauty.

And then...bubbles, from somewhere bubbles. Some fucker had brought along a bubble machine. Who? Why? I still to this day don't know. But why would you bring a bubble machine to a punk gig, when did soapy water ever belong at a punk gig? Were they trying to re-enact The Stones 'It's Only Rock & Roll' video? I don't know, but if they were, fuck off.

Bubbles everywhere, flying through the air, settling on the raving ones, sinking into that precious, hallowed, sticky, unwashed floor. It was more than the floor good bear. It didn't know how to cope with soapy suds. Down went the dancers, down went the moshers.

'Turn that bloody thing off!' somebody shouted. And they shouted at us but it wasn't our bubble machine, how do you turn it off?

A group of grappling girls slide along the front of the stage. Hey collide with Eagle sending out to his back. He's winded and bawls the rest of the song out siting on the edge of the stage — his miraculously corrected.

'Turn it off!' more a desperate pleading than a command now.

Someone guessed, had a go, and got it wrong — a tide of bubbles shoots out across the hall, mayhem ensues.

Carrying on regardless, I kick into the next song as billows of bubbles rise before the stage obscuring the fallen and stricken. Suddenly the drums stop — Fozz never stops, he was famous for never stopping — is he being responsible now? No of course not he's a drummer. I watch Fozz launch himself from the top of his drum kit, he flies across the stage out into the soapy fray. He disappears from view. There's a loud crack. Followed by a low groan. We've stopped playing.

Jon steps forward, trips over unseen soapy skinhead and goes down but the bass is held aloft, saved. But my mic-stand is felled by a Mohawk and goes over, BANG! There are sparks shooting everywhere, bouncing off the ceiling and into the crowd. The lights go out, the floor clears in an instant as the crowd takes shelter balancing on the pews, thank the gods people still smoked, out came the lighters.

The bubbles dissolved and there's Fozz looking like a question mark, staring at his own leg that seems to be wrapped around his neck.

'I think my legs broken.'

'No shit Fozz.'

'Fuck him he played with Hawkwind,' somebody reminded us.

And here it comes…

'Hold on it's only my right one. I can finish the gig.'

And he did. The lefty bastard played six more songs and was then carried out—crowd surfed out – like a fallen hero, down the stairs to a waiting ambulance, to the cries of 'Hawkwind twat!'

On came the lights and the remainder of SPOG climbed back onto the stage to take a bow, only to discover that somehow in the crush to carry out our idiot drummer someone had fallen against Jon's 'Dean' bass. The neck had snapped in half, no one owned up. I don't blame them. He's a big bastard.

Nine months later. Eagle had a new band whose was so bad they made him look good. Jon had picked up a paint brush and was making money painting animal portraits and Fozz had broken his other leg by falling out of a chair.

I was a Dad again—I had to sell the guitar and so returned to writing. People can't sing along to short stories but writers are seldom electrocuted by their laptops, so I'm good. The Indian Queen finally shut up shop two years later. It's now a terribly trendy bar for the well-dressed stiffs who like their music programmed, and the kids who need it loud have nowhere to go. Inglorious days indeed, but every now and then I bump into someone who says, 'weren't you in that band, what happened to you guys?'

And I offer to buy them a pint and I say, let's sit down and let me tell you the story, and it's all true.

BIOGRAPHIES

MIKE FIORITO'S most recent book, Call Me Guido, was published in 2019 by Ovunque Siamo Press. Call Me Guido explores three generations of an Italian-American family through the lens of the Italian song tradition.

Mike's short story collections, Hallucinating Huxley and Freud's Haberdashery Habit, were published by Alien Buddha Press.

Mike has had fiction, nonfiction and poetry published in Ovunque Siamo, Narratively, Mad Swirl, Pif Magazine, The Honest Ulsterman, Chagrin River Review, The New Engagement and many other publications.

He is currently an Associate Editor for Mad Swirl Magazine.

NICOLA HUMPHREYS is a part-time writer with a full-time job to pay the bills. She writes short stories of connections and a sense of belonging, on her blog aramblingcollective.wordpress.com

Published in several anthologies and on-line journals, including the Saboteur shortlisted 'No Good Deed' by Retreat West. Nicola has almost finished writing her debut novel, 'Polytechnic'.

All of her dresses have pockets.

NICHOLAS KARAVATOS is a poet who often performs in spontaneous collaboration with musicians.

A graduate of Humboldt State University in Arcata and New College of California in San Francisco, he taught creative writing from 2006 through 2017 at American University of Sharjah in the United Arab Emirates. In spring 2018, he was a US Ambassador's Distinguished Scholar to Ethiopia.

POETKEN JONES is an organic original from the poetry and music scenes of 1980s Austin. Publishing in underground zines and reading in front of bands before becoming front man for the band Peace Corps (Early name Peace Corpse, finally Peace Corp), he released numerous independent projects, some of which were reviewed in Maximum Rock and Roll, Sound Choice, Option, and other local and national forums. PoetKen has performed at dozens of legendary Austin Venues on 6th street and beyond including the Ritz Theatre, Steamboat, and the Beach Cabaret. Jones' latest book The Way Life Goes: PoetKen Song Lyrics 1980s was released December 2019.

The kid (**GINA LASPINA**) has been exposed to the hc/punk world since birth. Her father is an old school hxc,Straight Edge,Vegan skater who has set her on her path into hxc & punk. She is a gifted artist and lives by her convictions.

JASON O'TOOLE is the author of Spear of Stars (The Red Salon, 2018) and the forthcoming Soulless Heavens. He has been featured in An Anthology of Poems from The Red Salon (2018) and We've Seen the Same Horizon (2019). His writing has appeared in Heathen Harvest Periodical, Nixes Mate Review, Tigershark, The Asylum and other publications. He was the vocalist for the NY Hardcore Punk band, Life's Blood. He performed as the featured poet for the National Poetry Month event at Lovecraft Arts & Sciences accompanied by musician Alec K. Redfearn.

MICHAEL ALLEN POTTER is a poet, playwright, editor, and memoirist who holds degrees in English and creative writing from Union College (New York), San Francisco State University, and The University of Iowa.

His work has been published widely in journals and anthologies in the US, the UK, and in Canada and he has taught creative nonfiction at Union College, The University of Iowa, and at The Just Buffalo Literary Center.

Find him: icartographer.wordpress.com

NEIL S. REDDY is an ex-guitarist but continuous lover of live music. Writer of two collections of twisted short stories and two novellas published by Weasel Press. Based in the UK—used to be called underground now just independent and wondering what the difference is.

WEASEL is a queer author and The Dude of Weasel Press. His latest book, *Cut the Loss*, was released in July of 2019.

OTHER TITLES FROM WEASEL PRESS

Pan's Saxophone by Jonel Abellanosa
Hyper-Real Reboots by Sudeep Adhikari
despair is a mandelbrot set by sudeep adhikari
Wayward Realm by Sendokidu Adomi
Ghost Train by Matt Borczon
To Burn in Torturous Algorithms by Heath Brougher
Klonopin Meets Sisyphus by Adam Levon Brown
Harmonious Anarchy by Matthew David Campbell
H A I L by Stanford Cheung
Young Thieves in a Growing Orchard by Samuel E. Cole
Talk Like Jazz by Joseph Cooper
The Madness of Empty Spaces by David E. Cowen
The Seven Yards of Sorrow by David E. Cowen
Bleeding Saffron by David E. Cowen
Face Down in the Leaves by Dwale
Wine Country by Robin Wyatt Dunn
City, Psychonaut by Robin Wyatt Dunn
Dark is a Color of the Day by Robin Wyatt Dunn
Smash & Grab Poems by Ryan Quinn Flanagan
In Winter's Dreams We Wake by Ryan Quinn Flanagan
Improbable...Never Impossible by Vixyy Fox
Reach for the Sky by Vixyy Fox
The Night at the End of the Tunnel or Isaiah Can You See? By Mark Greenside
Brinwood by RK Gold
Just Under the Sky by RK Gold
Civilized Beasts Vol I-III edited by Laura Govednik
If the Hero of Time was Black by Ashley Harris
Furry Haiku edited by Thurston Howl
Dormant Volcano by Ken Jones
Email Epistles by Ken Jones
In and of Blood by Kat Lewis
Purple Fantasies by Gary Mielo
Evergreen by Sarah Frances Moran
I Am A Terrorist by Sarah Frances Moran

Death & Heartbreak by Leah Mueller
I'll Only Write Poems for You by Max Mundan
Rising from the Ashes by Meghan O'Hern
Lipstick Stained Masculinity by Mason O'Hern
Chaos Songs by Scott Thomas Outlar
Viscera by Manna Plourde
Ribbon and Leviathan by Manna Plourde
In Another Life, Maybe by Michael Prihoda
the first breath you take after giving up by Michael Prihoda
the same that happened yesterday by Michael Prihoda
Beneath this Planetarium by Michael Prihoda
Years without Room by Michael Prihoda
Toast is Just Bread that Put Up A Fight by Emily Ramser
I forgot How To Write When They Diagnosed Me by Emily Ramser
Conjuring Her by Emily Ramser
UHAUL: A Collection of Lesbian Love Poems by Emily Ramser
The Escape by Rayah
Miffed and Peeved in the UK by Neil S. Reddy
Taxi Sam in PINK NOIR by Neil S. Reddy
Not Kafka: A Collection of Ugly Shorts by Neil S. Reddy
Tales in Liquid Time by Neil S. Reddy
Inevitable by Amy L. Sasser
Satan's Sweethearts by Marge Simon and Mary Turzillo
Taste I Say, You're Timeless by Chuck Taylor
Jazz at the End of the Night by Weasel
Cut the Loss by Weasel
We Don't Make It Out Alive by Weasel
Time Passes Like Flames in the Distance by Weasel
Vagabonds: Anthology of the Mad Ones edited by Weasel
Passing Through edited by Weasel
How Well You Walk Through Madness edited by Weasel
Colliding with Orion by Chris Wise
Wolf: An Epic and Other Poems by Z.M. Wise
Kosmish and the Horned Ones by Z.M. Wise

Coming Soon from Weasel Press

Going Somewhere by Joe 3.0
What Makes a Witch by Linnea Capps
Book of Beasts by Holly Day
The Moon Crawls on All Fours by Robin Gow
My Name Does Not Belong To Me by Luke Kuzmish
Things for Which You Thirst by Claudine Nash
Dire Moon Cartoons by John Sullivan
Horror Before It Was Cool edited by Jonathan W. Thurston
Once More with Noise by Weasel
Nothing Nice to Say by Stephanie Webber

www.ingramcontent.com/pod-product-compliance
Lightning Source LLC
Chambersburg PA
CBHW060354050426
42449CB00011B/2986